BY THE SEASHORE

by Helen Orme

ticktock MEDIA

Copyright © **ticktock Entertainment Ltd 2003**
First published in Great Britain in 2003 by ticktock Media Ltd.,
Unit 2, Orchard Business Centre, North Farm Road, Tunbridge Wells, Kent, TN2 3XF.

We would like to thank:
Nick Owen, Duncan Matthews at the Blue Planet Aquarium and Elizabeth Wiggans.
Illustrations by Simon Clare Creative Workshop.

Picture Credits:
Alamy images: 6-7, 8-9, 10-11, 12-13, 16-17, 20-21, 22-23, 26, 28-29.
Corbis: 1, 14-15, 24-25, 30-31, OBC.

Every effort has been made to trace the copyright holders, and we apologize in advance for any unintentional omissions.
We would be pleased to insert the appropriate acknowledgements in any subsequent edition of this publication.

ISBN 1 86007 351 4 pbk
ISBN 1 86007 341 7 hbk
Printed in Hong Kong

Contents

All words appearing in the text in bold, **like this**, are explained in the glossary.

Think...

What do sea creatures eat?

How do they protect themselves?

How do they move around?

The sea is home to thousands of creatures—fish, **crustaceans**, and **mammals**. Some live on the seashore, and some live in the oceans. Many birds live near the sea, too. They eat the other creatures that live there.

Imagine...

How would it feel to be a creature living under the sea?

Aaghhh!

It looks like you are about to find out...

5

This is a jellyfish.

Jellyfish live in every ocean in the world. Some even live in fresh water. A jellyfish has no head, no brain, no heart, and no bones.

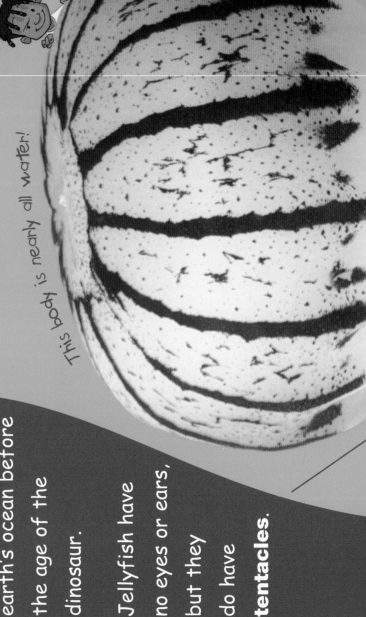

This body is nearly all water!

Jellyfish have been around for over 600 million years. There were even jellyfish in the earth's ocean before the age of the dinosaur.

Jellyfish have no eyes or ears, but they do have **tentacles.**

Don't sting me!

Jellyfish use their tentacles to find food. Some jellyfish have tentacles that could stretch halfway down a soccer field!

Each tentacle has thousands of tiny stinging cells.

Some jellyfish stings are so strong that they make people feel ill.

When a tentacle touches another creature, stinging **cells** explode and push **barbed** stingers and poison into the creature's flesh.

Even a tentacle that has been torn off of a jellyfish can sting.

7

watch out!

This creature is hungry.

It's a starfish.

Starfish live in oceans all over the world.
There are more than 1,500 different types.
Starfish are not really fish. They are
echinoderms. Unlike fish,
starfish do not have
backbones. But they
do have arms
called *rays*.

Most starfish have five rays.

If a ray breaks off, a new one will grow.

Starfish wrap their rays around the shells of **prey,** such as clams and mussels. Then they pull them apart.

Starfish can turn their stomachs inside out. Then they push them inside the shells of other creatures so they can eat them!

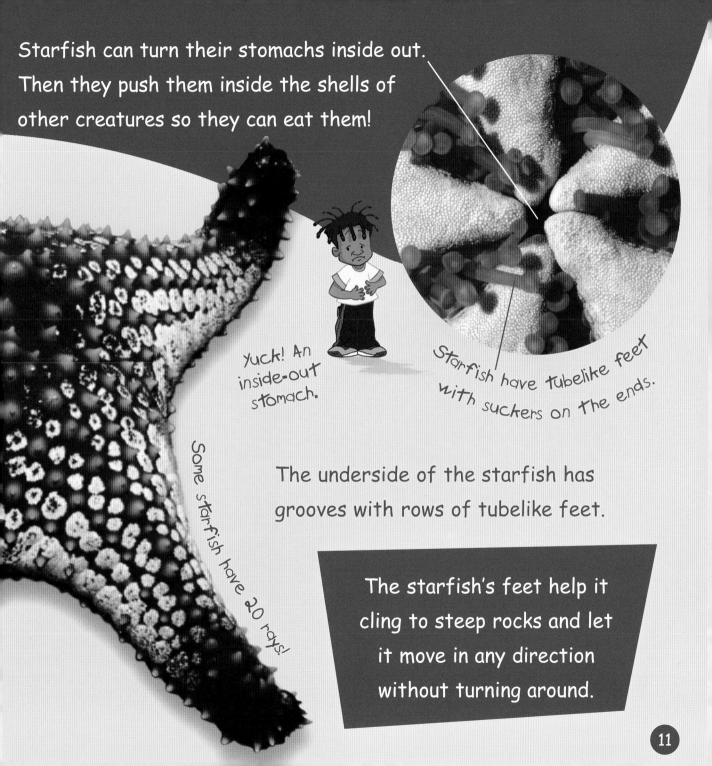

Yuck! An inside-out stomach.

Starfish have tubelike feet with suckers on the ends.

Some starfish have 20 rays!

The underside of the starfish has grooves with rows of tubelike feet.

The starfish's feet help it cling to steep rocks and let it move in any direction without turning around.

This is a mantis shrimp.

Mantis shrimps are highly-skilled **predators**.
They live in warm seas across the world
and hide in burrows on seabeds
or in holes in **coral reefs**.

This is a peacock mantis shrimp.

Their feeding arms move as fast as bullets!

SMASHER!

There are two types of mantis shrimps: spearers and smashers. This one is a smasher!

Walking legs

Spearers stab passing fish with their claws, while smashers can shatter small animal bones. Smashers can even break the thick, strong glass of an aquarium tank.

Shrimps can see lots of different colors that human beings cannot see. Their eyes can even look in different directions at the same time.

Shrimps don't have skeletons. Their bodies have a covering of tough **chitin**. As they grow, shrimps molt. They lose their old skin and grow new skin.

Each eye can turn and look in every direction: forward, backward, left, and right!

Swimming legs

Male fiddler crabs use their giant claw to fight other male crabs and to attract females.

This crab gets its name because people think that its large claw looks like a violin, or fiddle.

When the crab moves its large claw, it looks as if it is playing the fiddle!

This is a **fiddler crab**.

Fiddler crabs live together in mud or sand burrows (holes) on the shore. They make front doors for their burrows out of balls of mud; this keeps water out. All male fiddler crabs have one giant claw and one tiny one.

Females and young crabs have two small claws.

Some fiddler crabs are right-clawed (with big right claws) and some are left-clawed!

Ahhh! I'm stuck!

Is it a sea monster?

No! It's an octopus.

Octopuses are found in oceans all over the world. They can live near the surface or in water as deep as the length of a football field. They most commonly eat crabs. They can crack the crab shells open with their strong beak-like mouths.

An octopus has eight arms, called tentacles

The mouth is here, underneath the skirt

To hide from enemies, an octopus can quickly change its skin color and texture to match its background. It can also squirt dark ink from its body so predators cannot see where it is!

The powerful **suckers** on the tentacles help the octopus hold on to its prey and move along the seabed quickly.

Each tentacle has two rows of suckers.

The giant octopus can grow up to 9 metres across or as long as a school bus.

Octopuses in aquariums have been known to escape from locked tanks and to find their way around mazes to get food treats or to bite human beings!

Sea horse bodies have a protective covering of bony rings. Because the rings are so heavy, sea horses are poor swimmers.

Sea horse eyes can look in different directions at the same time.

They swim by moving this special fin on their backs.

These spines protect them from **predators**.

The female sea horse lays eggs in a special pouch on the male's front. The male then gives birth to the baby sea horses.

These are sea horses.

Sea horses are really fish. There are over 30 different types, and they all live in warm or **temperate** water. They have snout-like mouths that they use to suck up the tiny animals that they eat from the water.

Sea horses have no teeth.

Sea horse tails are very strong.

Sea horses can hold onto things with their tails. This stops them from getting swept away by strong **currents** in the water.

Pelicans have very special beaks. The birds scoop up large amounts of seawater, then squeeze out the liquid, leaving the fish behind.

The beak has a large pouch hanging underneath it.

Pelicans can grow up to four feet tall which is as big as a goat!

Dalmatian pelicans keep their eggs warm by holding them on their **webbed** feet. But if pelicans are disturbed, they jump up, and the eggs can roll off and break!

This is a dalmatian pelican.

Dalmatian pelicans are amongst the rarest birds in the world. They live across Asia and eastern Europe, but there may be fewer than 6,000 left. They are very large birds, and are powerful fliers and swimmers.

They have wingspans of up to ten feet, which is wider than a car!

What's for lunch?

Dalmatian pelicans have a simple way of feeding their young—they just open their mouths! The chicks put their whole heads inside to collect their meals of fish.

This is a sea otter.

Sea otters live on the west coast of the U.S. between California and Alaska. They commonly eat shellfish and other sea creatures. To open shells, sea otters float on their backs with the shellfish balanced on their stomachs. Then they hammer the shell with a stone until it breaks.

Sea otters can close their ears and noses when they are underwater.

Otters have special flaps of skin under their front paws that help them hold their food.

Sea otters usually float. They even sleep floating on their backs!

The sea otter's back legs are shaped like **flippers**. These help the otter swim.

A delicious shrimp dinner!

To stop themselves from floating away, sea otters wrap long strings of kelp (a type of seaweed) around their bodies.

Sea otters are **mammals**. They have the thickest fur in the animal kingdom. For many years hunters killed sea otters for their fur. Now it is against the law to hunt them in most places.

Who owns
these whiskers?

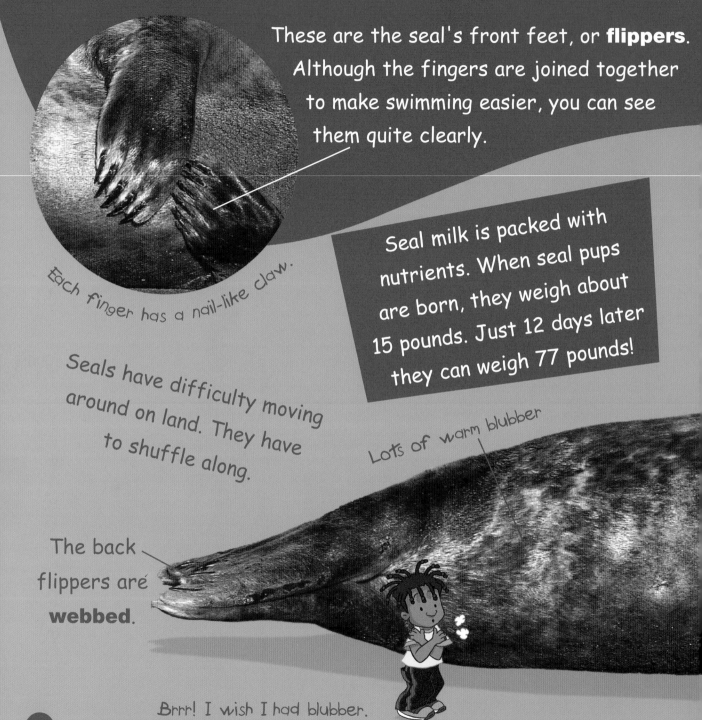

These are the seal's front feet, or **flippers**. Although the fingers are joined together to make swimming easier, you can see them quite clearly.

Each finger has a nail-like claw.

Seal milk is packed with nutrients. When seal pups are born, they weigh about 15 pounds. Just 12 days later they can weigh 77 pounds!

Seals have difficulty moving around on land. They have to shuffle along.

Lots of warm blubber

The back flippers are **webbed**.

Brrr! I wish I had blubber.

It's a seal.

Seals are **mammals**. Most types of seals live in cold places. Their bodies have a thick layer of fat called *blubber* to keep them warm. Seals love to eat fish, shellfish, shrimps, octopuses, and squids.

Seals have **streamlined** bodies. They are among the world's best divers and can reach high speeds in the water.

These whiskers are used to detect fish up to 164 yards away!

You can swim fast when you are streamlined.

GLOSSARY

BARBED Something with small, sharp hooks.

CELLS Tiny parts of an animal's body. People, animals, and plants are made of cells.

CHITIN A hard substance similar to the materials that hair and fingernails are made of.

CORAL REEFS Colonies of thousands of tiny animals called *polyps*. They produce hard outer skeletons for themselves that join together to make a reef.

CRUSTACEANS Animals like crabs, lobsters, and shrimps. They have a hard outer skin, jointed bodies and limbs, but no skeletons. Most live in the water.

CURRENTS Movements of water.

ECHINODERMS Animals with armlike body parts that point outward from the center of their bodies like bicycle spokes. Many have spiny skins.

FLIPPERS Animal arms or legs that are flattened, like paddles, for swimming.

MAMMALS Animals with warm blood that produce milk for their young.

PREDATORS Animals that live by killing and eating other animals.

PREY Animals that are killed and eaten by other animals.

STREAMLINED Something with a smooth shape and skin. A streamlined animal can move easily through the air or through water.

SUCKERS Parts of an animal that let it hold on or stick to things.

TEMPERATE Not too hot or too cold.

TENTACLES Parts of an animal's body that can be used for touching and holding things. They look a bit like arms.

WEBBED Webbed feet have skin between the toes to help with swimming.

INDEX